Lisa-Sophie Schöben

Aus der Reihe: e-fellows.net stipendiaten-wissen

e-fellows.net (Hrsg.)

Band 1485

Superstition. Nothing Is Incredible Enough Not to Be Believed In

GRIN Publishing

Bibliographic information published by the German National Library:

The German National Library lists this publication in the National Bibliography; detailed bibliographic data are available on the Internet at http://dnb.dnb.de .

Imprint:

Copyright © 2012 GRIN Verlag, Open Publishing GmbH
Print and binding: Books on Demand GmbH, Norderstedt Germany
ISBN: 978-3-668-01339-1

This book at GRIN:

http://www.grin.com/en/e-book/300986/superstition-nothing-is-incredible-enough-not-to-be-believed-in

GRIN - Your knowledge has value

Since its foundation in 1998, GRIN has specialized in publishing academic texts by students, college teachers and other academics as e-book and printed book. The website www.grin.com is an ideal platform for presenting term papers, final papers, scientific essays, dissertations and specialist books.

Visit us on the internet:

http://www.grin.com/

http://www.facebook.com/grincom

http://www.twitter.com/grin_com

Nothing Is Incredible Enough Not to Be Believed In

Lisa Schöben

Jahrgangsstufe 12, EN/11

Content

1 Introduction

"Superstition is the weakness of the human mind;

it is inherent in that mind; it has always been

and always will be."

Frederick the Great[1]

It is really true that superstition has already had a long tradition. Its roots can be traced back into Ancient Greece; it played an important role in antiquity and had its peak in the Middle Ages which is especially known for the witchcraft trials. Many tragedies, dramas, and poems from that period of time dealing with superstition are still popular today.

By definition "superstition is a widely held but irrational belief in supernatural influences, especially as leading to good or bad luck, or a practice based on such a belief."[2] It attributes powers to persons and things which are not nature-given.

Is superstition a current matter nowadays? Which elements are still present today and how far is it spread? Is there room for anything so old-fashioned, credulous, and primitive in our modern, rational time determined by reason, intellect, and sanity? Or is it just an unimportant "fashion" which recurs every now and then and is only smiled at by the majority? Does superstition have any significance other than entertaining us? What do superstitious rites include and what traditions are still exerted today?

2 Superstition

2.1. What Is "Superstition"?

"In fact men will fight for a superstition quite as quickly as

for a living truth – often more so, since a superstition is so

intangible you cannot get at it to refute it, but truth is a point

of view, and so is changeable."

- Hypatia[3]

The term "superstition" comes from the Latin word "superstitio" which means "craze" and the Greek word "deisdemonia" which can be translated as "fear of the gods". It is a steady temptation for everyone who tends to stop asking questions easily, who mixes or gives up religious belief in favour of more manageable practices and handier "being in the know". Single phenomena of conventional belief are absolutized, perverted, and cultivated. Superstition attributes strength to things and persons that are not nature-given and so is a substitute trust in "things" which protect life instead of religion – abundantly unconsciously hidden behind many mechanisms, rites, and customs.

Otmar Schnurr differentiates two different forms of superstition:

1) Public superstition is based on very old customs which have developed and been handed down from people who were directly connected with nature. They had experienced the natural powers and introduced rites to soothe the forces.
2) Art superstition is a result of secret arts and occult sciences which are based on speculations.

Superstition needs to be taken seriously and understood as an indicator of deeply felt human needs. It is an attitude against the traditional belief.[4]

2.2. The Origin of Superstition

Forms of superstition are based on the experience with IN-security and UN-faith. The fascination of it originates from need of speculation, the human liability to secrecy and from the unappeasable urge to obtain knowledge. Knowledge gives power – even over the uncertainty and the menacing, but it can also develop neuroses. Quiet, introverted, insecure persons are especially endangered. This is most notable when they isolate themselves. Church bears also part of the blame because to many, it is not a home anymore.

Five psychological roots of superstition can be categorized as follows:

1) Fear of the future, death, war, loss of job, and threatening illnesses which technical and medical aids do not suffice to conquer. Therefore people try to come to grips with their fear with the help of magic, God, the devil, or other mysterious forces and make them subservient.
2) Naïve devil fear is dated back to the time mankind did neither have knowledge about thunderstorms nor earthquakes nor medicine against diseases. That is why they blamed bad creatures, Satan, or other people who were said to be in relation with the devil due to their weird lifestyle or odd looks. Despite all scientific progress, this fear of deceitful powers has not died out.
3) The desire to know about the future is another root of superstition because not everyone has got the strength to live a life in the face of an uncertain future.
4) The longing for mysticism, ecstasy, and transcendency is another reason. The world we live in has become cold and "matter-of-factly". Thus teenagers often escape to

drugs to experience similar aspects like spiritism in which they come into touch with transcendence.

5) The last reason for the emerge of superstition is <u>cruelty, sadism, and aggression</u> which is based on the human instincts. "Witch-hunt" is an example of mankind living out its impulses at somebody else's expenses. The torture which is a part of sadism is the "playing field" of human aggressions and suppressed sexual wishes. Nowadays, we likewise have the "black masses".

All these aspects originate in the fun to experiment with the new and exceptional and the human desire for the mysterious, especially, when our world becomes more rational and the perspectives duller. But these causes of superstition can only be defeated by the victory of sanity.[5]

2.3. Superstitious Practices

2.3.1. Symbols of Good & Bad Luck
Even in today's modern world many symbols stand for good or bad luck. You can find many customs in everyday life such as crossing fingers, hanging a horseshoe over your door, catching a falling leave in fall, spitting over one's shoulder or throwing salt over your own shoulder. If you find a four-leaved clover or meet a chimney sweep, you are said to be a very lucky person.

There are also signs for bad luck. It is said that if a black cat crosses your way or if you break a mirror, you will have a bad fortune. Other omens for mischief are spilling salt, walking under a ladder, getting up on your left foot or if the horseshoe over your door turns around, your chance will fall out and you will be afflicted. Especially feared is the hoot of an owl because this is a death sign. For some people the simple number "13" is horrifying because it is reputed as an indicator of bad luck whereas in other regions like China or a small part of Brazil it is "the lucky number". In Mandarin, the digit "1" when positioned in tens sounds like the word "definite", while the digit "3" sounds like "life". As a result, the number "13" can mean "definitely vibrant" or "assured growth". Another tradition which is an anxiety-provoking aspiration for fortune are chain-letters. Supposedly, they bring happiness to those who follow the instructions and pass them on and bring harm to those who do not obey. Chain-letters are a promise and a threat.

Furthermore, men have always kept charms to protect themselves. There are active charms, so called talismans that are supposed to bring good luck and additionally passive charms, such as amulets or birthstones which are said to defeat harmful things.

On top of that, making a lot of noise is also a good way of keeping evil spirits away as is traditionally practiced at eve-of-the-wedding parties.[6]

2.3.2. Lucky Charms

Accidentally found lost property is assigned a special significance concerning the extraordinary manner of acquisition, both bringing good or bad luck. They can be a meaningful omen.[7]

2.3.3. Astrology

> *"In the sky, there is neither coincidence, nor approximately,*
>
> *nor wrong way, nor illusion, in contrast solemnly order, truth,*
>
> *reason, and continuance."*
>
> *Pythagoras*[8]

"Astrology" had its origin in Mesopotamia where it arose due to the geocentric worldview. It is also called "Speculative Astronomy" because it examines the cosmic impacts on men based on the interpretation of the relation between the stars and our earth just like the moon influences the ocean's tides. However, it is contradictory if the stars have any kind of power over mankind or if they can predict human existence. Still, it is the most wide spread form of fortune-telling in terms of horoscopes.[9] After all, Astrology can be influential as shown in this popular case: In the year 1524, astrologers predicted a second deluge due to the conjunction of the three planets Saturn, Jupiter, and Mars influenced by Pisces. The closer the time approached, the bigger the people's fear was. Emperor Charles V. was advised to consign his troops to a high mountain range and to set up huge warehouses. In Toulouse, there was even built an ark. Luther also thought this harmful constellation to be an emblem of God.

Though this is only an extraordinary example, the position of the stars is often observed to determine one's destiny.[10] Especially at the time of birth, the planets' constellation are said to have a great impact on a person's life which can promise wealth and stability or unfortunately suffering, poverty, and death.[11]

2.3.4. Dreams & Oneiromancy

The faith in prophetic and symbolic dreams which require interpretation has existed since antiquity. Dreams are seen as important connection inside humans between the sensual and the extrasensory world which burst through the familiar and accustomed reality and apparently belonging to another "reality". They are intuitions that pronounce something present or prospective.[12]

Dreams dealing with children or pieces of art stand for sorrow and grief, whereas tragedies warn you of great danger. White objects or a dead person who steals from you in your dream forecast a close friend's or relative's death. Water is interpreted as displeasure, dance as rage, and pearls as tears. Dreams of comedies mean that you will have to endure mocking.

On the contrary, a dream of barkeepers or tax collectors bode well, fire stands for big joice, and eggs bring good luck. If you dream of apples, you can expect joys of love and if you dream of lice, it means that you will gain a lot of money.[13]

Similar phenomena are visions, second sight, or apparitions.

2.3.5. Magic

Magic is defined as an action grounded in superstitious tendencies. It is used to reach something beneficial or to keep away everything unwanted and even to harm others.[14] It is the highest level of theosophy which describes the most intimate unity with God himself where a person himself is qualified to accomplish supernatural actions.[15] There are two forms of Magic: "theurgy" and "black magic". The used forces of theurgy belong to the natural order such as tricks, hypnotic influence, mind reading, and certain healing powers.[14] In contrast, black magic is grounded in the subjugation of evil spirits through mystic formulas and actions.[15]

2.4. Supernatural Creatures

2.4.1. The Devil

Satan is a creature of malice whose only effort exists in misleading men to commit a sin. His subordinates are demons. The devil emerged around 400 B.C. because it displeased men that God supposedly leads them into temptation.[16] In the late Middle Ages, people did not doubt the efficiency of supernatural practices. Their undisputed effect was assigned to different possibilities but their initiator was in every case of devilish origin. The "deal with the devil" is believed to be the premise of every superstitious initiative. Especially wizardry shows up demonic provenance in particular for predictions. On the contrary, angels have a protective function for men. They pull humans off evil forces and lead them to good.[17] Today evil takes shape through a person's will and actions.[16]

2.4.2. Vampires & Werewolves

Since antiquity, mankind has believed in creatures that torture him in service of the underworld. A person who was condemned from the legal community was said to turn into a wolfman. In ancient Rome, murderers had to wear a hat made out of wolfskin.

King Charles IV. (1316-1378) was reputedly a werewolf. In 1589, a man was executed near Cologne because it was attested that he had torn apart human bodies and eaten their brains while being in shape of a werewolf. A similar criminal was locked into a mental home in France nine years later. In Salzburg in 1717, five werewolves were punished with penalty of galleys for eight years and expatriation and in 1720 a werewolf was executed. This superstition lives on in Wallachia and the Balkan region.

A corpse of a supposed vampire was dug up and cut into pieces in Maravia in 1617. In 1732, thirteen vampires were spotted in Serbia. This extraordinary form of superstition still haunts Slavic peoples today.[18]

2.4.3. Witches

Witches cannot be assigned to a special social rank. "Witches" were often women who had an obvious advance in knowledge due to their experience in curing the sick. In former times, the female sex was in charge of child births. Women were midwives and doctors and were responsible for the people's health. That is the reason why she was blamed for diseases, impotence of men, dead births of babies, and commitment of newborns to the demons. A few hundred years later, only physicians with completed studies were allowed to work as doctors but only males were admitted to university.

The traditional woman's function was to be fertile and she had a reputation of having a magical connection with the fertility of the earth. This belief was based on the menstrual cycle which equals the lunar cycle, so men thought she had power over nature and the cosmic powers. Women were the ones who sowed the fields. Back in the days, it was only logical for the people that the one who charmed the harvest from the soil was also capable of destroying it. Due to their linking with the earth, women were accused of storms, bad harvests, the perish of cattle, and the ruin of foods and seeds.

Since Eva was thought to be a temptress, women were reputed to be outstandingly liable for every kind of vice and excesses. The so-called witches apparently had a magic salve through which they could fly if it was spread on the skin. With the aid of this product they flew to the "Blocksberg" to celebrate "covens" with excessive consumption of alcohol, inhalation of intoxicant fumes, naked round dances, and exhibitionistic acting out of their sexuality only for the sake of lust and appetite. In the Middle Ages, the faith in the "pact with the devil" existed. He was said to act through the witches.[19] Those women were equipped with practices and knowledge in the domain of spells concerning harm, healing, love, and weather. In the late Middle Ages, "magic" got the meaning of "harm spell"[20] what is probably the reason of the occurrence of the witch trials which had their peak at that time. A typical inquisition (in 1487) started with the denunciation of a person who supposedly was a witch or wizard whereby it was of great importance that the informer stayed anonymous. If you were accused, it was your death sentence. Witnesses were heard in court only as witnesses for the prosecution, never as witnesses for defence and their only condition was not to be the victim's archenemy. The first procedure was a simple interrogation whose single aim was to force the accused person to a confession. If the defendant did not admit his delict, the examination was followed by an "embarrassing questioning" which meant torture which ended deadly in every case.[19]

2.5. Superstition & Religion

Superstition contradicts the natural God-given order.[21] A child's trust is the original, blind trust. Adults however make conscious judgements of the reliability of a person and the trust has to intensify. This is always a risk and a gift. No human being can survive without trust and faith ultimately equals trust. Those who trust in God experience deep relief and a new spirit of life. With the help of faith, some insecurities are endurable.

Superstition is a bond service. The principle of freedom separates belief from superstition: men betakes himself from God's freedom into the slavery of the elements. Superstition hinders the possibility of religious trust to the loving God because one feels dependent on gods, spirits and forces whom one tries to calm.[22] Although superstition can be regarded as a symbol of paganism as relic of Pre-Christian times[23], the Church is not innocent concerning the fact that supernatural property has spread so far. When the faith in God vanishes, even Christians are and will be vulnerable to superstition.

In the 10th century B.C., people believed in the Bible which says that there are neither good nor bad forces. The relationship between God and the humans is depicted as a close contact. However, in the last two centuries B.C. God is shown as the "remote one" and the space between Him and us is filled with his angels who have the function of messengers. This development is important for the evolution of a personified might of darkness. It started with the question where quilt, disease, death, and eventually evil comes from. The answer people have found in the Bible is that evil does not come from God. It is caused by men's free will (➔lapse)[24]. From the Christian point of view, diseases were accepted as a godly punishment or test that could only be revoked by God. Seeking aid for hardships and sicknesses in supernatural practices equals hence violation of the alliance with God because help and refuge is not sought in God.[25]

Similar to the Christian belief superstition contains a faith in a temporary state after death; the spirit world, in which the soul is being prepared either for heaven or hell. This is the explanation why spirits such as ghosts, angels, and even Satan have a human-like shape because they used to be humans.[26]

3 Superstition In Shakespeare's "Macbeth"

In Shakespearian time the Englishmen and the Scots believed in supernatural beings like demons, ghosts, and witches. The so-called "wise women" played an important role in society because they healed the sick, predicted the future, and had good luck charms. But when the harvest failed or someone died, the search for the cause was often solved by accusing the wise women of having used magic to cause harm. They were killed because they were said to have entered a pact with the devil what provided them with demonic magical power. In return, the devil received their souls. This belief in devil-worship included women flying through the air to meet in deserted places by night to worship and have sex with the devil, and commit terrible crimes, like killing babies, cooking and eating them.

The most popular supporter of devil-worship was King James I. of England, the former King James VI. of Scotland. In 1597, he published a book on superstition called "Demonology", that should extinguish every doubt in the existence of witches. Already in 1563, the Parliament of Edinburgh declared wizardry a capital crime which was the basis for prosecutions, tortures, and burnings.

With his work "Macbeth" which is loaded with spook and the supernatural, Shakespeare flattered the art-loving, superstition-obsessed king who later graciously supported the author's group of actors with financial aids so that they called themselves "The King's Men" since 1603. In his tribute to the king, Shakespeare did not only acknowledge King James' fascination with the supernatural but also praised his virtues and presented him as the ideal king through the character of Banquo.

The most important part of supernatural powers in "Macbeth" is the group of the three witches. From the first moment on, the Thane of Glamis is unconsciously engrossed of the weird sisters what is shown through his first words: "So foul and fair…"[27] which repeats the witches' spell from Act I/Scene 1. The weird sisters never make a secret out of how evil they are. As evil as they might be, they never lie to Macbeth. They rather let him perish due to their ambiguous messages which evoke his ambition for power. Thus, the witches are the stimulating force of actions and forces of fate. Their prophecies cause the tragedy to begin and the evil deed to get into a tangle. They stand for inscrutable fate and represent the bad might itself; the dark, sinister side of nature. The weird sisters are responsible for the social rise and moral decline of the Macbeths' and as they are no women but hybrids[28], they are just as unnatural as the people's destinies. Eventually, Macbeth is subject to Satan.

Already Act I/Scene 1 presents chaos and disorder in the three different spheres of life: the state, nature, and the supernatural. Nearly each scene has references to unnatural occurrences: darkness during day time, horses eating each other, and owls killing falcons[29]. The question of the first witch whether they should meet in thunder, lightening, or rain hints at the Elizabethan belief in the supernatural power of witches to influence the weather whereas the second and third sister are able to predict the time of their next meeting. The term "hurly-burly" implies turmoil, war, and rebellion in society. They make paradoxical statements about the outcome of the battle and about the inverted order of good and evil in the world. Furthermore, they hint at the infected air which is polluted by smoke, dirt, and water, and contaminated by their own presence because devil is in possession of their souls which grants them magical power for example to move through the air and to get to any place below the moon. The weird sisters are attended by their personal demons, also called familiars, which take the shape of animals such as toads or cats[30].

Additional supernatural phenomena are the dagger that leads Macbeth to Duncan's chamber[31], Banquo's ghost at the banquet[32], as well as Lady Macbeth's hands spotted with imaginary blood[33].

4 Modern Superstition

4.1. Superstition In The 20th Century

A survey in Germany that was published in the "Stern"-magazine in August 1986 shows that there is still a belief in supernatural incidents or actions. 93% of all German citizens believe in things between heaven and earth which sciences cannot explain. Two thirds of them have already experienced something themselves that could not be explained by sanity. 34% of all questioned people think it is possible that humans exist who can use magic to help or harm others. 70% of all participants believe in "white magic" or the possibility of healing the sick even when the doctors cannot help anymore and in the opinion of 66% clairvoyance is a potential phenomenon.[34]

New-Age-Movements developed in the 20th century and they are based on the spiritual poverty in modern times and the wide-spread tune of the "Last Days". Some rudiments originate in the Christian thought of "Invert!".

Through "Rosemary's Baby" (a movie from 1968) Satanism has gained popularity. Christian sins are vices in Satanism. According to his followers, Satan embodies the true wisdom because all these sins lead to physical, psychological, and emotional satisfaction. This is the point at which superstition becomes a threat for our existence. The four murders at a Rolling Stones concert in 1969 prove this.

The first satanic church was opened six years earlier in San Francisco. At the same time, an English band called "Black Sabbath" invented a new kind of stage show at which hard rock music is illustrated through black masses, devil evocations, and witch cult. They functioned as role model for the Heavy-Metal-Scene but over the time violence has been replaced by fear of the unknown. Many members of famous bands have reported that they are trance-like while they are playing on stage. They seem to be obsessed and feel as if they do not play but are rather watching themselves play.

Another group that worships cruelty are the "Hell's Angels" who have renounced themselves from society. They are often related to criminal activities such as arms deal, drug dealing, racketeering, and prostitution.

Ozzy Osbourne used to bite off birds' heads at his detestable live shows until he accidently bit off the head of a bat someone had thrown on stage. He is a devotee of Aleister Crowley (1875-1947) who is reputed to be the greatest Satanist of the 20th century. Apparently, the magician had a vision in 1896 saying he was the "Antichrist". During his lifetime, he thought he was being used as communication device to the Mankind by an occult might. His aim was to become the ruler of the world by taking possession of the demons' powers. He practices black magic and Satanism, and included intense usage of drugs and sexual captures and aberrations in his acts of sexual magic. His "teachings" became a new path, a new mentality, and a new religion for many spiritual groups who flourished in Europe and the United States after World War II.

Erich von Däniken is another superstition-lover. He tries with passion to create a new world view and he knows he will gain resonance because the leaning towards the bizarre is very strong these days.

If played backwards, "Stairway to Heaven" by the band "Led Zeppelin" is a coded confession of faith to Satan. This technique of hiding messages is called "backwards masking" and is not possible to be decoded with an ordinary music player. If one listens carefully at the backwards played song one can understand the following: "Listen! We have been there... I will sing, because I live with Satan... Serve me! ...There is no escaping it... with Satan... if we've got to live for Satan... Master Satan..."[35]

4.2 Superstition In Modern Literature Using The Example of "The Vampire Diaries"

In contemporary literature, we can find many elements of superstition. Books like "Harry Potter", The "Twilight" series, "The Vampire Diaries", the "House of Night" series and many more are so popular that they have been turned into movies and television series which also delight in great popularity. I decided to choose "The Vampire Diaries" series as example because it includes a wide range of supernatural practices and phenomena.

Through the use of flashbacks, the viewer is set back into the Middle Ages now and then. The couple Mikael and Esther is presented this way. She was a witch and to protect their family, husband and wife decided to turn themselves and their six children into vampires. To complete this magic she used "The Original Petrova's" blood. Though the "Original Vampire" family now was very powerful and strong, the vampire race that had been created has several weaknesses. In changing her family into supernatural beings, Esther interfered in the natural order and thus had to fear consequences. Vampires cannot enter places inhabited by humans without being asked to come in, they are vulnerable to sunlight and vervain and bloodlust is their utmost desire and often takes control over their bodies.

One of their children, Niklaus (often simply called "Klaus") is the most important vampire of the family and he is known as "The Original Vampire" even though he is not only a vampire but a hybrid; he is both vampire AND werewolf. As he became too powerful a witch cursed him by forcing his werewolf-side to become inactive wherefore she also used "The Original Petrova's" blood. Klaus' intent is to break the curse and become the creator of a new supernatural race that would threaten werewolves and vampires equally. To break the curse, he needs a witch to channel power of the full moon to release the spell of the "Moonstone" which binds it. He needs to sacrifice a werewolf by taking out his heart and a vampire by stabbing a wooden stake through his heart at the birthplace of the "Doppelgänger" and spill their blood on the "Moonstone". Additionally, he has to drink the "Doppelgänger's" blood until the point of death to become a hybrid. To break this curse, Klaus made up the legend of "The Sun and The Moon Curse" in order to have the help of the vampires and the werewolves to search the "Moonstone" and the "Doppelgänger". "The Sun and The Moon Curse" makes vampires powerless against the sun and werewolves unable to transform unless there is a full moon. According to the invented legend, vampires can move freely in the sunlight during daytime when the curse is lifted by a vampire while werewolves remain dependent on the moon but if the curse is broken by a werewolf their race will be able to turn at will and remain in control of their actions while the vampires will forever be slaves to the sun. Once Klaus manages to break his curse he changes werewolves into vampires in order to create a "hybrid race" but for the complete change he needs once again the "Doppelgänger's" blood.

"The Doppelgänger" is a woman of the Petrova family line who is specifically created as a means to break the real curse. There is the "Original Petrova", then Katerina Petrova (or

Katherine Pierce), the first "Doppelgänger" who changed herself into a vampire to not be sacrificed and "survive" and Elena Gilbert, the second "Doppelgänger" and protagonist of the story. All three women look identically though one never gets to know the "Original Petrova". To break his curse, Klaus needs Elena because she is human and thus can be sacrificed while Katherine is a vampire and therefore already dead.

A vampire is created when a human dies and still has vampire blood in his organism after having drunk or having been forced to drink vampire blood. When the person resurrects he has the choice whether he wants to die or drink human blood to finish the transition. A vampire needs blood to survive that does not necessarily need to be fresh human blood though it is the most nutritious and most strengthening but animal blood and stored blood is also sufficient. When they do not get blood over a longer period of time, vampires dry out and are neutralized which means that they cannot move or act; but can be revitalized through blood. Only wooden objects like stakes or bullets if stabbed through their hearts or werewolf bites are life-threatening whereby the latter can be healed with the "Original Vampire's" blood. Vervain and the sun can cause serious burns but most vampires possess a "magic ring" which allows them to move in the sunlight. Vervain is the vampire's most common weakness. Their special ability is to manipulate thoughts of humans and supernatural creatures unless the opposite consumed vervain or carries the herb close to his body for example enclosed in jewellery. Other gifts are a well-functioning ear with which they can listen from far distances, great strength and supernatural speed. The older a vampire is, the stronger he gets. Consequently, the "Original Vampires" are the strongest. They can only be neutralized with the help of a special "White Oak Ash Dagger".

In contrast to the vampires' creation, a werewolf is genetically predetermined and genes are hereditable. The werewolf-side of a potential werewolf remains dormant until he incurs guilt through a murder or a deadly accident that he caused. As soon as the werewolf-side has awakened, the person changes at every full moon which is very painful and cannot be controlled just as little as the actions completed in the shape of an animal which are controlled by the instinct of hunting vampires. That is why werewolves usually lock themselves and chain up during full moon. They are also very fast and strong, even while in human shape but they are only competitive to vampires at full moon.

The third species presented in "The Vampire Diaries" are witches as servants of nature. They possess magical abilities and with the help of the "Grimoires", a record of spells, rituals, herbs, etc. a witch can even step into contact with dead witches to channel some of their powers or to seek advice. Furthermore, there are three magic objects introduced in the series that were created by witches: a silver talisman, the "Gilbert compass", and the "Gilbert ring". The silver talisman belonged to Esther and she uses it from the "otherworld" to interfere in this world. To stop her intrusion a witch destroyed the necklace but it reconstructed the damage itself and appears to be intact and unharmed again.

"The Gilbert compass" was originally a simple pocket watch but after having found the missing magical part it helps to locate vampires.

The last object is the "Gilbert ring" which protects its human wearer from supernatural forces and thus grants immortality.[36]

5 Conclusion

In conclusion, one can say that superstition still is a current issue in our time though it is not commonly practiced anymore and mainly found in entertainment rather than in everyday life. But there are always exceptions like the various occult groups I referred to on the pages 11/12. On the other hand, the great majority of modern persons is only interested in learning something about different elements of superstition in fictional books or movies. However, the main purpose of superstition is amusement and the supernatural powers and practices are not taken seriously. Many customs and traditions are unconsciously, and by most unknowingly, performed and passed on, for example a lucky penny, wishing good luck, or crossing fingers.

I enjoyed working on this topic very much and learning about a dateless part of human culture which still influences the life of many people all over the world.

Bibliography

1   Baumann, Karin: Aberglaube für Laien I. Zur Programmatik und Überlieferung
    spätmittelalterlicher Superstitionenkritik. Königshausen & Neumann, Würzburg
    1989
2   Böck, Christine; Neubauer, Martin: Macbeth. William Shakespeare. Mentor Verlag
    GmbH, München 2005
3   Bologne, Jean Claude: Magie und Aberglaube im Mittelalter. Von der Fackel zum
    Scheiterhaufen. Patmos Verlag GmbH & Co. KG, Düsseldorf 2003
4   Plec, Julie; Williamson, Kevin: "The Vampire Diaries" television series based on
    the books by Lisa J. Smith
5   Schnurr, Otmar: Aberglaube. Faszination und Versuchung. Kösel-Verlag GmbH &
    Co., München 1988
6   Scott, Robert Owens: Lektürehilfen William Shakespeare "Macbeth". Ernst Klett
    Verlag für Wissen und Bildung GmbH, Stuttgart 1991
7   Shakespeare, William: Macbeth. Cambridge University Press, Cambridge 2010

8   Stemplinger, Eduard: Antiker Aberglaube in modernen Ausstrahlungen.
    Dieterich'sche Verlagsbuchhandlung m.b.H., Leipzig 1922

Internet: http://vampirediaries.wikia.com (30.04.2012)

Footnotes

1 http://thinkexist.com/quotation/superstition_is_the_weakness_of_the_human_mind-it/165493.html (30.04.2012)

2 www.oxforddicitonaries.com (30.04.2012)

3 http://www.brainyquote.com/quotes/authors/h/hypatia.html (30.04.2012)

4 Schnurr, O.: page 12-14, 21, 112, 114

5 Schnurr, O.: page 16f., 23, 38f., 95, 112

6 Schnurr, O.: page 9, 47, 51

7 Baumann, K.: page 466f.

8 Stemplinger, E.: page 599

9 Schnurr, O.: page 28ff.

10 Stemplinger, E.: page 111

11 Baumann, K.: page 289

12 Schnurr, O.: page 40

13 Stemplinger, E.: page 34f.

14 Schnurr, O.: page 47

15 Stemplinger, E.: page 58

16 Schnurr, O.: page 70ff.

17 Baumann, K.: page 292, 314f.

18 Stemplinger, E.: page 62, 92

19 Schnurr, O.: page 54-60

20 Baumann, K.: page 440f.

21 Baumann, K.: page 372f.

22 Schnurr, O.: page 19, 22f.

23 Baumann, K.: page 468

24 Schnurr, O.: page 19, 69f.

25 Baumann, K.: page 440f.

26 Schnurr, O.: page 35

27 Shakespeare, W.: I,3 l. 36

28 Shakespeare, W.: I,3 ll. 43-45

29 Shakespeare, W.: II,4

30 Shakespeare, W.: I,1

31 Shakespeare, W.: II,1

32 Shakespeare, W.: III,4

33 Shakespeare, W.: V,1

34 Schnurr, O.: page 10f.

35 Schnurr, O.: page 74f., 81-87, 101,105

36 "The Vampire Diaries" television series